8/10/2022

Goals for 2022-2023 school year

1. Develop effective strategy for ESL → Algebra courses

2.

Made in the USA
Middletown, DE
14 June 2022